AFFIRMING CA

GW01398715

Christopher Irvine

MAKING
PRESENT

The Practice of
Catholic Life and Liturgy

DARTON·LONGMAN+TODD

Published by Darton, Longman and Todd, 1 Spencer Court, 140–142 Wandsworth High Street, London SW18 4JJ in association with Affirming Catholicism, St Mary-le-Bow, Cheapside, London EC2V 6AU

ISBN 0–232–52094–1

The views expressed in this booklet are those of the author and do not necessarily reflect any policy of Affirming Catholicism

Booklets designed by Bet Ayer, phototypeset by Intype, London and printed by Halstan and Co Ltd, Amersham, Bucks

CONTENTS

Affirming Catholicism

Affirming Catholicism has never been, and is not intended to be, yet another 'party' within the Church of England or the Anglican Communion but rather a movement of encouragement and hope.

A group of lay people and clergy met together in 1990 to identify that authentic Catholic tradition within the Church which appeared to be under threat. Wider support was expressed at a public meeting on 9 June 1990 in London and at a residential conference in York in July 1991.

Since then Affirming Catholicism has been afforded charitable status. The following statement is extracted from the Trust Deed:

> It is the conviction of many that a respect for scholarship and free enquiry has been characteristic of the Church of England and of the Churches of the wider Anglican Communion from earliest times and is fully consistent with the status of those Churches as part of the Holy Catholic Church. It is desired to establish a charitable educational foundation which will be true both to those characteristics and to the Catholic tradition within Anglicanism . . . The object of the foundation shall be the advancement of education in the doctrines and the historical development of the Church of England and the Churches of the wider Anglican Communion, as held by those professing to stand within the Catholic tradition.

In furtherance of these aims and objectives, Affirming Catholicism is producing this series of booklets. The series will encompass two sets of books: one set will attempt to present a clear, well-argued Catholic viewpoint on issues of debate facing the Church at any given time; the other set will cover traditional doctrinal themes. The editor of the series is Jeffrey John; the first four titles in the series were: *Imagining Jesus – An Introduction to the Incarnation* by Lewis Ayres; *Why Women Priests? – The Ordination of Women and the Apostolic Ministry* by Jonathan Sedgwick; *History, Tradition and Change – Church History and the Development of Doctrine* by Peter Hinchliff; *'Permanent, Faithful, Stable' – Christian Same-sex Partnerships* by Jeffrey John. Other titles are: *Politics and the Faith Today – Catholic Social Vision for the 1990s* by Kenneth Leech; *Christ in Ten Thousand Places – A Catholic Perspective on Christian Encounter with Other Faiths* by Michael Ipgrave; *Is the Anglican Church Catholic? – The Catholicity of Anglicanism* by Vincent Strudwick; *Lay Presidency at the Eucharist?* by H. Benedict Green.

To order these publications individually or on subscription, or for enquiries regarding the aims and activities of Affirming Catholicism write to:

The Secretary
Mainstream
St Mary-le-Bow
Cheapside
London EC2V 6AU

Tel: 071–329 4070

Worship at the Centre

The Catholic movement in the Church of England has always given a high priority to worship in the life and work of the Church. The present danger is that Catholic-minded Christians in a plural and multi-faith society will retreat into the sacred precincts and become absorbed in an agenda of churchy affairs. This is a danger which must be strenuously resisted, not least because, as I intend to show, such a retreat cuts against the very grain of Catholic liturgical life. Approached from the opposite angle, the question could be asked as to whether worship should occupy such a central place in the life of the Church at a time when personal and social needs are becoming increasingly visible and pressing in our contemporary world with all its unjust disparities and violent disjunctions. To sharpen the question: should the Church deploy so many resources, time and expertise on maintaining the round of liturgical worship when so many demands are being made on its ministry, and new opportunities for mission are presenting themselves? To face these questions (and face them we must) we need to examine the basis of the privileged position of worship in the life and work of the Church.

The first, but not necessarily the most important, plank supporting the privileged position of worship concerns our very identity as Anglicans, or how we define and understand ourselves. The first person to set out a coherent understanding of the Church of England, defined over against both the Roman and other Churches of the Reformation, was the sixteenth-century bishop, Jewel of Salisbury. In his *Apologia Ecclesiae Anglicanae* (1562), Jewel presented the Church of England as an essentially 'liturgical church'. Its foundation deeds are not a confession of beliefs or a set of doctrinal statements, as in some other Churches of the Reformation, but a Book of Common Prayer, the historic threefold ministry of bishops, priests, and deacons, and the Gospel sacraments of baptism and eucharist. Historically speaking, it could be said that the very taproot of Anglicanism, the feature that gives it its place in the family of Christian Churches and its distinctive character, is its ordering of corporate forms of worship. It has often been said: if you want to see what Anglicans believe, see how they worship.

Secondly, a prominent Conservative Evangelical scholar was quoted in a recent edition of the *Church Times* saying, 'If we get our theology right, it will lead to praise.' Worship, in other words, is the consequence of 'correct' doctrine. This view effectively reverses the classic principle of *lex orandi, lex credendi*, the principle that worship establishes belief, that worship is the source and origin of Christian doctrine. In the traditional understanding, it is precisely in our response to the One whose name is invoked and whose gracious initiatives are commemorated in worship, that the reality of God is apprehended and known. How God comes to be known could be explained in terms of mystery: specifically, the mystery of God himself, who dwells in unapproachable light; the mystery of God's saving plan revealed in Christ; and the 'holy mysteries' of the Church's sacramental celebrations. In and through acts of worship the divine mystery impinges upon worshippers, bringing them into contact with the saving work of Christ, objectively and historically shown in the coming and fate of the historic Jesus, and made present in the Church's corporate prayer and sacramental celebrations. It is this sense of the mystery of Christian worship, of the palpable presence of the divine mystery in the unfolding of the drama of Christian worship, which was caught by Ambrose of Milan when he exclaimed to God, 'I find you in your mysteries'. The same point has been cogently made in more recent times by the liturgical theologian Aidan Kavanagh. In his book *On Liturgical Theology* (Pueblo, 1984), Kavanagh argues that worship, as the occasion of encounter with the divine reality, is 'primary theology'. Consequently, he explains, all who engage in the activity of worship are engaging in 'primary theology'. He goes on to say that this primary theology needs to be coherently ordered and articulated, that is, subjected to the kind of intellectual activity which we generally associate with the word theology. But this is rightly seen to be a secondary activity, and Kavanagh's special contribution is his reminder that worship is theology, the source and touchstone of our knowledge of God. If worship is the impetus of primary theology, then its privileged position in the life and work of the Church rests, at least in part, upon the fact that it is the very source and impulse of all Christian thought, feeling, and action.

Thirdly, it could be argued that worship informs the Church's mission. It shows something of what Christians are called to be and do beyond the institutional Church. In looking beyond the bounds of Christian community, we might well be assisted by the teaching of Fr. Herbert Kelly, the founder of the Society of the Sacred Mission, an Anglican religious community for men. Kelly, an ecumenist and educational pioneer, was convinced that the whole Christian venture was to discern and promote the grace of God in the world. On spreading a newspaper open, he would say, (for the benefit, of course, of those within earshot), 'Well, what's God up to today?' He firmly believed that God was to be found in every sphere of human life and activity, and vehemently resisted attempts in Christian thought and piety to place God exclusively in the 'religious' compartment of life. However, the repeated emphasis in his teaching on the need to discern and co-operate with the divine will in every arena of life was not intended to devalue or subordinate the activity of prayer and worship. On the contrary he suggests that the very activity and structures of worship provide the key for unlocking the mystery of God's presence in the world. In a kind of stock-taking exercise to clarify the aims and outlook of his 'sacred mission', Kelly wrote: 'We were well aware that you must find Christ in the Church before you will find him anywhere else, but the two are not the same . . . The worship of the parish church is the key which should unlock the mystery of God in the world (*Ad filios*, 1920). In other words, worship is the prime occasion when Christians can be awakened to the divine presence and begin to grasp, and be grasped by, the pattern of God's dealings and purposes for us and his world. Furthermore, through this recognition of the saving drama of God, the paschal mystery of Christ's death and resurrection, set forth in the words, symbols and ritual actions of Christian worship, worshippers are enabled to discern and respond to the divine presence in the little deaths and resurrections of our everyday experience.

The Greek word for liturgy, *leitourgia*, means both worship and Christian service. This dual meaning is symbolically enacted in the two most basic liturgical acts: first, the 'coming together' as a worshipping assembly, and secondly, the dismissal and dispersal of the community at the end of an act of worship. At the end of the liturgy, the assembled worshippers are formally dismissed: 'Go in peace, to love and serve the Lord'. The congregation disperses into the wider communities to which they belong and within which they are to exercise their vocation to discern and celebrate the graced moments and occasions in the lives of those communities. Again, when the worshippers 'come together', they are gathered in the name of the triune God, and the needs and concerns of the wider world are brought and voiced in the prayer of the worshipping community. So, in the very rhythm of worshippers coming together and being sent out 'to live and work to (God's) praise and glory', we see that liturgy and life are inextricably linked together. In the light of this and the other points which have been sketched out here, we are constrained to conclude that the privileged position of worship in the Christian endeavour is secured by the fact that worship, and probably worship alone, can generate, direct and correct both a truly Christian life and the life of the Church, in and for the world.

The Components of Worship

It is probably true to say that more liturgical material has been written in the last thirty years than at any other period in the history of the Western Church. The Second Vatican Council in the early 1960s ordered a radical revision of the rites of the Roman Catholic Church, and even now we await the publication of a new English translation of the missal. The first Liturgical Commission of the Church of England was set up in 1955, and the compilation and production of liturgical texts has been fairly relentless since the 1960s. The cynic might say that the literary quality of liturgical writing has deteriorated in inverse proportion to the proliferation of texts, although some recent productions (not least *Promise of His Glory* and *Lent, Holy Week and Easter*) count against such a view.

As we move towards the year 2000 and the end of *The Alternative Service Book*'s synodically designated life span, liturgical revision and its attendant cluster of linguistic and doctrinal issues will again become a prominent matter in the Church of England. There are positive signs that the present Liturgical Commission will be well placed, not least because of the various consultations arranged by PRAXIS, to hear the views expressed across the whole of its constituency. There are now, for instance, good channels of communication between members of the Commission and the Prayer Book Society, and a new appreciation has emerged of the importance of retaining some traditional texts for use in Sunday worship.[1] At the other end of the spectrum, as it were, it is extraordinary that the *Alternative Service Book (1980)* appeared at the time when people were becoming ever more conscious of the way in which language affects the way we relate to each other. The kind of language we use indicates the kind of social world which we wish to construct and inhabit, and the complaint that the repeated use of the words 'men' and 'mankind' makes women feel excluded needs to be reckoned with. Underlying this problem of exclusive language is the more serious challenge to the Church, the contention that such language reinforces the patriarchal structures of society, which suppress and dominate women. Those who attempt to write liturgy in a contemporary idiom cannot duck the issue of inclusive language, and happily the Liturgical Commission has handled the matter in a sensitive and sensible manner in its report *Making Women Visible*

(Church House Publishing 1989). The Bishop of Winchester, Colin James, wrote in the Preface to the report: '... in the longer term the way forward lies in attempting a proper balance between male and female in new liturgical work rather than *ad hoc* adaptations of existing texts.' What might count as a 'proper balance' is open to question. Clearly the debate is open, and the issues surrounding inclusive language are far from being resolved to everyone's satisfaction.

Apart from the avoidance of excessive use of masculine pronouns, and possibly a certain amount of linguistic adjustment to make liturgical language more inclusive of women, there is also the question of the way we image God, and the metaphors we employ to depict the divine reality. In the writings of the mystics we are reminded that God transcends our imaginings and cannot be caught by the words we spin or the concepts we construct, and it is a salutary reminder. Our talk of God, and the language we use to invoke and address the divine Trinity in worship, is quite inadequate to the task. As someone once said, the reason we repeat the word holy in the 'Holy, holy, holy' is not because of the paucity of our vocabulary, but because God is ineffable. The point to be drawn here is that portions of our liturgical prayer need to be answered by silence. At particular points, the very language we use should deliberately lead us into moments of still silence. Silence is a necessary complement to the language we use in worship, and our recognition of the inadequacy of that language underscores its significance. The language of worship matters, and matters more than we might suppose. For the Word was made flesh so that we might come to speak his words, and furthermore, it is through speaking those words in prayer that our relationship with God is expressed and realised. In the voicing of prayer worshippers enter into the experience of the One who, anointed with the Spirit, cried 'Abba, Father', and realise their status as adopted children of God, sisters and brothers of the eternal Son. Words spoken cannot be retrieved, and words addressed to another are the most potent means of maintaining and deepening a relationship. It is imperative to remember that the language of prayer is essentially the language of address, and a call into relationship with the Trinity of Love, of the most disturbing passion and gentle kindness.

As the language of address, liturgical language needs to be evocative and expressive in its tone, rhythm and vocabulary. Writers of liturgy ought to avoid the pitfall of using didactic language, or writing flat, descriptive prose. But in a plural society which is conscious of the relativity of cultures and given the prevalence of the visual image over the written word, how are we to address God? The term 'Almighty' is derived from the Byzantine concept of God as 'Pantocrator', literally, one who rules over all, and how can we call God almighty in a world which is beset by the issues of domination, power and powerlessness? Such a question does more than expose the cultural dissonance between ourselves and fifth-century Greek Christians: it reminds liturgists that their task involves more than merely recovering in an archaeological way the riches of a past tradition. Attempts to forge a different nomenclature for God have resulted in expressions such as 'Creator God', or 'Loving Wisdom', which have the advantage of not designating a gender, but risk a rather impersonal understanding of God. Clearly the difficulties in composing adjectival attributes for God are considerable, but perhaps it is possible to enumerate some principles to guide us through the particular pitfalls and challenges of liturgical writing in contemporary language.

The first concerns the literary character and usage of liturgical language. Poetry has the ability to shock, stretch and stimulate new ways of thinking and feeling, and contemporary religious poetry, such as the work of Kathleen Raine or Elizabeth Jennings, can undoubtedly nourish the individual's sense of God and suggest a vocabulary to express that sense of the divine. But poetry, even in a contemporary idiom, cannot serve as a vehicle for the official worship texts of the Church. Liturgical language is public language, language which is spoken either by a sole voice or as a chorus in a large assembly of people in the resonant setting of a church or cathedral. Language used in such a context must avoid esoteric expressions and needs to be cast in a form which can be repeatedly spoken aloud. In this respect liturgical language needs to be deliberately written as oral language and requires a certain character of durability, a form which can be spoken, perhaps daily, without coming to sound trite or hollow. The point is that contemporary liturgical writing, though distinct from poetry as such, needs to be poetic.

The second principle which ought to guide our liturgical writing is that liturgical language is the language of 'common prayer'. This is not to say that it should be devoid of any literary merit, or that its vocabulary and syntax should be such as to make it immediately accessible for all, but more radically, that it should have a public resonance, the capacity to give voice to our general human aspirations and fears, hopes and disappointments.

The third guiding principle is that liturgical writing needs to be faithful to the tradition, the tradition encapsulated in ancient liturgical texts and the biblical writings. This is not in itself a restrictive measure. On the contrary, all writers write within a tradition, and the best have no qualms in borrowing from earlier writers (as T. S. Eliot, for instance, plundered the work of Julian of Norwich and Lancelot Andrewes). To say that liturgists must work from within a tradition is to say that in some respects their writing is a re-writing. But it is a re-writing which gives ample scope for the contemporary Christian imagination, and when imagination is used it will avoid the dangers of producing archeologisms, such as the phrase 'revealed the resurrection by rising to new life', which can strike the ear of the worshipper as 'theology-speak', or the simple 'parroting' of Scripture. To risk an example of what it might mean to write out of tradition, rather than merely re-stating it, we could think of an antiphon or refrain for the Venite (Psalm 95), the opening psalm of Morning Prayer. We could use a phrase from the psalm itself, but this would be to parrot Scripture. On the other hand, we could construct a phrase such as: 'The Lord makes darkness and light, and has raised the Sun of Justice: O come let us worship him.' This refrain is a new composition, yet clearly utilises imagery from both Scripture and early Christian writing, and furthermore manages to capture something of the theology of daily prayer.

Here is a final observation on this third guiding principle. It is interesting to note that the Liturgical Commission's report *Patterns for Worship*, unlike the seasonal resource books *Lent, Holy Week and Easter* and *Promise of His Glory*, was not well received by either the House of Bishops or the General Synod. Perhaps the reason for the unenthusiastic reception was that most of the material it contains was not written out of earlier worshipping traditions of the Church, as the material in the other two volumes clearly was. As a result it strikes the reader as comparatively artificial and rootless.

There is, of course, much more that could be said about the topic of liturgical language, but at a time when liturgical texts are proliferating we especially need reminding that worship is not only the speaking and hearing of words, but a rich commerce in symbols and gestures. Instructive here are the tales of some who on entering the church on a Sunday morning are given two separate books and three sheets of photocopied paper, and dream of being liberated from the printed text. There is a primary need for all of us to appreciate how God becomes present for and with us, not only in words spoken and heard, but also in what is seen and felt, touched and tasted, in the sacramental celebrations of the people of God. For these reasons, I want to discuss at greater length and detail the symbolic character of worship.

Symbol and ritual

> The people who really live by the liturgy will come to learn that the bodily movements, the actions, and the material objects which it employs are all of the highest significance. It offers great opportunities of expression, of knowledge, and of spiritual experience; it is emancipating in its action, and capable of presenting a truth far more strongly and convincingly than can the mere word of mouth.[2]

These words of Romano Guardini, who was one of the pioneers of the twentieth-century Liturgical Movement, are a necessary corrective for those who view worship as a purely verbal affair, an activity solely concerned with the reading or singing of words. Of course, liturgical texts are crucially important, and the words we say and sing are vital components of worship, but liturgy is primarily an action, something we do. To put it another way, we could say that in an act of worship things are said and things are done.

Prayers, for instance, are both said and embodied, as we assume different bodily postures for different kinds of prayer. We might kneel or bow our heads for the prayer of confession, and stand for the thanksgiving prayer. Indeed, from the moment people enter the church building until the end of the liturgy, there is continuous movement, despite the fact that so often worshippers are inhibited by fixed and serried ranks of chairs or pews, whose very arrangement unfortunately suggests that the role of the people of God in worship is to sit and listen.

Most of the liturgical action centres around the altar, the ambo, or lectern, and the font, and it is specifically the actions surrounding the declaiming of the Word, the taking and giving of the eucharistic bread and cup, and the pouring of water, to which Guardini draws our attention. Furthermore, he asserts that it is precisely these symbols and ritual gestures which are eloquently expressive of our commerce with the triune God and with each other within the context of the worshipping assembly. The problem, it seems, is that the language of symbols has largely become a forgotten language, or at best only a half-remembered one. The reasons for this state of affairs are multiple, and an attempt to analyse this 'crisis of symbolism' would be a complicated business. This crisis particularly inflicts and debilitates Western Christians, and in his writings the theologian Paul Tillich admitted that within his own religious tradition the neglect and suppression of the symbolic had diminished the ability of those who belonged to that tradition to apprehend and handle the riches of religious truth. The roots of the problem are very deep and affect the ways in which we construct our understanding of the world, that is, of what we consider to be real, and the grounds upon which we might regard anything to be true. At this point we are brought face to face with a hard-nosed, no-nonsense empiricism, which will only allow those things which can by physically verified and manipulated to count as being real, and will regard descriptive, factual language as being the only reliable form of communication. Closely allied to this outlook is the utilitarian attitude which will only assign value to those things which are of practical and immediate use; things, as we might say, which are purposeful and productive. Given the difficult social and economic conditions in which some people live, it is entirely reasonable to place a premium upon pragmatism, but it is possible that reality might be deeper and wider than what we concede to be real, and it would be inhuman, if not immoral, especially in a time of mass unemployment, to assess the meaning of our lives solely in terms of obvious, practical usefulness. There are, after all, many activities which are vital for the living of a human life, but which serve no immediate practical and material purpose: time spent admiring a piece of art, listening to a piece of music, or simply exchanging gossip with a friend. The value which is placed on practical usefulness is economically driven, but this must not lead us to disregard and undervalue those activities which appear to serve no practical purpose. Some of those activities might well bring us into contact with realities which are far greater than our world of making, getting and spending – realities which are hinted at and brought into play by artistic and religious symbols.

Guardini, too, identified an attitude of utilitarian pragmaticism as a serious impediment to the worshippers' full engagement with the business of worship, which he described in a marvellously suggestive phrase, 'the wondrous playfulness of liturgy'. This, of course, is serious play: through the complex symbol system of worship we are to play, as the Orthodox say, 'heaven on earth'. The challenge to those who would worship is whether they are sufficiently open and receptive to the dimensions of reality conveyed to us by the use of symbolic objects and actions. For many in our churches it might require no more than raising the eyes from the printed page of the service book, in order that they might more readily catch the sights and sounds of the liturgy; the movement, colour of vestments, breaking of bread, and flowing of baptismal water. For those who plan, regulate and perform the Church's public worship the challenges are even greater. In the view of the social anthropologist Mary Douglas it is the ecclesiastical decision-makers who have failed to grasp the full significance of the symbolic dimension in worship and social life, and it is they who receive the full blast of her critique. Considering the reforms implemented by the Roman Catholic Church after the Second Vatican Council, Douglas ventures to say that 'those who are responsible for ecclesiastical decisions are only too likely to have been made, by the manner of their education, insensitive to non-verbal signals and dull to their meaning. This is central to the difficulties of Christianity today. It is as if the liturgical signal boxes were manned by colour-blind signalmen.'[3]

This same failure on the part of the theological and ecclesiastical establishment to register the importance of the symbolic was laconically recorded by the depth psychologist Carl G. Jung. In his *Memories, Dreams, Reflections* he castigates a theologian who had come to him for psychoanalysis for his refusal to recognise the correspondence between the symbolic imagery which he found in the biblical texts, which were the objects of his professional study, and the symbolic forms which coalesced in his unconscious mind and surfaced in his dreams.[4] More generally, Jung observed that worshipping Christians had a special opportunity to live what he designated the 'symbolic life', but as he wistfully remarked, too few Christians actually took that opportunity. This reluctance to engage the 'symbolic life' springs, according to Jung's analysis, from a refusal on the part of the worshipper to hold together the half-known world of worship, and the everyday world of conscious effort and unconscious dreams.

If contemporary worshippers feel a little disheartened by the verdict that they suffer from a dulled symbolic consciousness, some consolation can be found in the fact that Christians living in the last decade of the twentieth century are not alone in being earthbound and literalistic. It seems that even the first disciples of Jesus sometimes failed to grasp the point that their teacher, that teller of parables and spinner of stories and similes, was getting at. There is an intriguing exchange between Jesus and the disciples recorded in Mark's Gospel, which reveals their singular inability to think metaphorically and raise their sights above the pragmatic level:

> Now they had forgotten to bring bread; and they had only one loaf with them in the boat. And he cautioned them, saying, 'Take heed, beware of the leaven of the Pharisees and the leaven of Herod.' And they discussed with one another saying, 'We have no bread.' And being aware of it, Jesus said to them, 'Why do you discuss the fact that you have no bread? Do you not yet perceive or understand? Are your hearts hardened? Having eyes do you not see, and having ears do you not hear?' (8:14–18, RSV)

It would seem that a crass literalism is seriously detrimental to our capacity to apprehend Christian truth, and that our refusal to engage with the symbols of Christian worship is a serious obstacle to the power of that worship to inform the worshipper's outlook and attitudes. In other words, our insensitivity to the symbolic in the drama of Christian worship can all too easily result in the kind of dislocation, lamented by Jung, between Christian liturgy and Christian life.

The so-called 'crisis of symbolism' is a challenge to us to recover a sense of the necessity of the symbolic dimension of worship and to sharpen our sensitivity to the way we handle symbols and embody their meaning in the ritual dance of the liturgy. But if we seriously wish to increase our symbolic competence and develop a greater appreciation of the symbolic character of worship, then we cannot duck the fact that we are dealing with a rather vague and nebulous concept. After all, according to the ways in which we commonly use the word 'symbol', any object or action can carry a symbolic meaning, in so far as it can stand for, represent, or denote something else. In the context of a discussion on the nature of worship we need to qualify this definition and attempt to say more specifically what we are talking about when we speak of symbols. It will help if we differentiate between different forms of symbolic communication, and arrange them on a kind of interpretative grid.

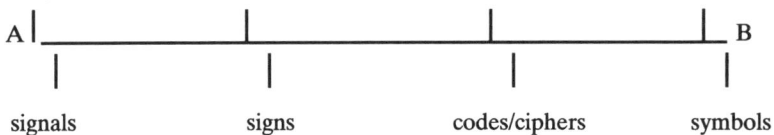

A |_____|_____|_____| B
  | | | |

  signals   signs   codes/ciphers   symbols

The diagram shows, from A to B, a sliding scale ranging from signals, through different kinds of signs, to codes and ciphers, and ending with what I would simply denote as symbols 'proper'.

What are the different forms of symbolic communication? The first, a signal, is a shorthand form of communication, and because it indicates a single command, or warning (like the ringing of the school bell to indicate a change of lesson, or the sounding of an ambulance siren to clear a way through the traffic), it is essentially a precise form of communication, an unambiguous sign demanding an immediate response.

Signs, however, belong to a more general category, and it is possible to distinguish between natural and conventional signs. A natural sign is essentially a 'sign of' something else, which is invariably a consequence of the signifier. So, for example, we might say that dark clouds are a sign of rain. The point to register is that there is a direct correspondence between the signifier and the signified; though in terms of our example, it should also be noted that the appearance of dark clouds on the horizon does not in every instance mean that it will rain. So, as we move from signals to natural signs we are shifting to a less precise mode of communication. Apart from natural signs, there are also conventional signs, where something is agreed to act as a 'sign for' something else. A good example of a conventional sign is a road or traffic sign, and in these cases it is clear that the information conveyed needs to be fairly specific, but the crucial point about conventional signs is that their meaning has to be learnt. We need to study the highway code and learn that the road sign indicating 'road works ahead' means just that (and not a person having difficulty with an umbrella, which it rather resembles). In other words, a 'sign for' is essentially representative (this stands for that), and because, at least in theory, we could change its meaning (by official agreement and a mammoth public education campaign), its meaning is arbitrary.

Codes and ciphers are a more complex mode of symbolic communication. A good example is a musical score, with its complex of notes, bar lines, time signatures, and so on, which indicate the scale and rhythm of the music. The single musician or orchestra has to perform the score, to translate the sequence of dots and lines into music, and interestingly no two performances of a single piece of music are entirely the same in sound. The point, as with the performance of any text, is that it has to be interpreted, and so we could say that its meaning is less fixed or precise.

Thus to return to our diagram, as we move through the scale from point A to point B, from signal to symbol, we shift from a point of precision to points of greater ambiguity. A symbol is much more ambiguous than a signal, and unlike a conventional sign, its meaning is not arbitrary. Sacramental symbols like oil, bread, wine and water are in one sense natural, and in another 'given'. They are 'given' in so far as they are historically rooted – for example we use water for baptism because Jesus was baptised in the waters of the Jordan, and we use bread and wine at the eucharist because when Jesus was at supper with his disciples he took bread and a cup of wine. These symbols are 'natural' in so far as the elements themselves evoke the purposes which they sacramentally effect, for oil soothes and heals; water cleanses and revives us, and literally breaks from the womb as a new human being is born into the world; bread and wine, elements of food and drink, are ingested, and thereby become a natural symbol of indwelling and communion.

However, the natural associations and historical origins of the elements of sacramental celebration do not exhaust their meaning, for as symbols, as distinguished from signs which have a one-to-one correspondence with what is signified, they are essentially ambiguous, and evoke and express a whole range of meanings. Furthermore, precisely because symbols are multivalent, they also appeal to, and invite a response from, the various levels of our being. A symbol can appeal to the emotions, trigger the imagination, resonate with the archetypal forms of the unconscious, and also be of cognitive significance. Such a range of possibilities precludes symbols from being regarded as being merely illustrative, representational, or even decorative.

When we think of signs, on the other hand, we think of something which signifies something else, so that what is signified is signified by a foreign form. This essential disjunction between the sign in itself and what it represents has led sacramental theologians to make the most convoluted attempts to jump the distance between 'sign' and 'signified' – the doctrine of transubstantiation being a case in point. This has had a curious effect upon the Christian imagination which, paradoxically, spins poetry celebrating the sacramental presence of Christ as though he were not present, as, for example, the words of the hymn *O esca viatorum*:

> O Jesu, by thee bidden,
> We here adore thee, hidden
> 'Neath forms of bread and wine.
> Grant when the veil is riven,
> We may behold, in heaven,
> Thy countenance divine.
> (*The New English Hymnal* No 300, verse 3)

My preference for the term 'symbol' as the most appropriate term for what in Catholic theology is generally called a sacramental sign, lies in the capacity of a symbol to evoke and express multiple levels of meaning. In so doing, the symbol invites us to participate in deeper levels of reality. This understanding of the symbol's function is at least suggested, if not explicitly supported, by a range of contemporary theological reflection. A number of theologians as diverse in background and perspective as Paul Tillich and Alexander Schmemann have claimed that far from being illustrative, or functioning as a visual aid, the sacramental symbol makes present for the worshipper the reality of the divine presence and purpose, by conjoining the divine with the human, the heavenly with the earthly. It is a mode of communication, in other words, which is dependent upon and made possible by the incarnation of God in the life and fate of Jesus of Nazareth, making accessible 'that which was from the beginning, which we have heard, which we have seen with our eyes, which we have looked upon and touched with our hands' (1 John 1:1). The language of symbol is an extension of the logic of incarnation, which in the rather abstract terms of Chalcedon, was the perfect conjunction, without confusion or separation, of divine and human life in Jesus Christ.

The co-inherence of the divine and human life suggested by the christo-logical thinking of the Cappodocian Fathers and the Chalcedonian definition accords with the etymological meaning of the word symbol, derived from the Greek verb meaning 'to throw together', which implies the placing and holding together of parts to form an integrated whole. This correspondence between the meaning of the word symbol and the principle of the incarnation highlights the dynamic of sacramental worship.

In the history of Western theology there have been repeated attempts to define 'sacrament' with ever greater precision and to settle the number of individual sacraments. Perhaps the prize for the finest logic-chopping in sacramental theology ought to be awarded to the fourteenth-century Francis-can theologian Alexander of Hales, who distinguished between baptism and confirmation by saying that baptism conferred the 'fullness of sufficiency', and confirmation 'the fullness of abundance'. In marked contrast, the Chris-tian East has retained a more general sense of sacramentality, and its theo-logians have been happy to operate with the more suggestive and polyvalent category of symbol in their explications of sacramental worship. The narrower Western definition of sacraments as 'effective signs' tends to lead to a rather instrumental view which sees individual sacraments as 'things', as individual means of grace, rather than events, or the meeting of earthly and heavenly realities. The Orthodox tradition has maintained the more general sense of sacramentality, and has accorded sacramental symbols the fullest sacramental realism. The Orthodox theologian Alexander Schmemann has affirmed in the strongest possible terms the reality of the divine presence in the sacra-ments and argues that the sacramental symbol is epiphanous, that is, that it 'both manifests and communicates that which it manifests'.[5] Schmemann's assertion finds support in the conviction that sacramental worship is at one and the same time the work of God and the work of the worshipping community. Exactly how God is at work in the worshipping community is spelt out in terms of pneumatology, of the operation and work of the Holy Spirit, and he argues that the reality of the sacramental symbol is accomplished by the Holy Spirit.

A biblical basis for the theological argument that it is the Spirit which realises the sacramental symbol might well be found in the 'Bread of Life' discourse in the sixth chapter of John's Gospel. This discourse, which most commentators concede has some bearing upon eucharistic faith and practice, concludes with these words placed on the lips of Jesus: 'It is the spirit which gives life, the flesh is of no avail; the words that I have spoken to you are spirit and life.' However we might interpret these particular words, they support the contention that the eucharistic mystery concerns and involves both Christ and the Holy Spirit, 'the two hands of the Father', as John Chrysostom once suggested. Thus it is appropriate to invoke the Holy Spirit in the eucharistic prayer itself. (This invocation of the Spirit is technically termed the *epiclesis*.)

The narrative of the eucharistic prayer, like the Jewish *haggadah* rehearsed on the night of Passover, is a recital of God's saving acts, but the purpose of this recital is not simply a re-telling of the sacred story, but an articulation of the desire and expectation that the saving effects of those past events may impinge, here and now, upon the assembled worshippers. Thus, the prayer appeals to the Father to send the Holy Spirit upon the elements of bread and wine, that they might become for the praying community the very life and being of Christ himself: '. . . grant that by the power of your Holy Spirit these gifts of bread and wine may be to us his body and his blood' (first and second eucharistic prayers, ASB Rite A). It is important to say that this *epiclesis* need not be regarded as being 'consecratory', in the sense which we usually associate with this term, of there being a 'moment of consecration'. The very notion of a moment of consecration is alien to Orthodox eucharistic faith and practice, which regards the whole of the eucharistic prayer as consecratory, rather than any specific part or section of it. As we saw, Schmemann was careful to speak of the role of the Spirit in the eucharist as the *realising* of the sacramental symbol. The Spirit realises, or accomplishes, the sacramental presence, in order that the bread and cup may be a symbol of Christ's presence, a living symbol whereby his purposes are unfolded among, through and within the lives of those who participate in the celebration. In this sense the eucharist gifts can be understood as symbols of transformation.

The eucharistic gifts are symbols of transformation in a double sense: first, in so far as they are transformed from 'ordinary food and drink'; and secondly, because of the expressed expectation and intention that those who participate in the liturgical celebration and receive the sacred gifts will themselves be changed, transformed from being a mere aggregate of individuals to being the Body of Christ, a symbol of God's coming Kingdom. In terms of our eucharistic praying this finds expression in what is sometimes referred to as the second *epiclesis*. In the third eucharistic prayer of the ASB rite A, the President prays: 'Send the Holy Spirit upon your people', and continues by asking that the whole Church may be united in God's Kingdom. This example is couched in rather general terms, but the *epiclesis* in the eucharistic prayers of the early Church tended to be more specific in indicating the effects upon the praying community of participating in the eucharistic sacrifice. The unity of the Church was invariably a common theme, but the expectation that the worshippers would be strengthened in the truth, receive renewal and forgiveness, and a pledge of the fullness of life in God's Kingdom, were also specifically cited.

The invocation of the Holy Spirit in the eucharistic prayer importantly reminds us of our dependence on the Spirit in all our praying; it gives depth and meaning to our appreciation of sacramental symbols; and, vitally, it expresses the recognition that the worshipping assembly needs to change, to become more of a community of Christ, if it is to become an agent of transformation in the wider world. This hope that the eucharistic community may manifest something of God's Kingdom, and the recognition that the community itself needs to be changed, ought to be set out a little more fully and explicitly than is the case in our current eucharistic prayers.

The use of symbols
Earlier it was suggested that a sign stands, logically or analogically, for something else, whereas a sacramental symbol manifests what it communicates to us, and communicates the reality it depicts. A sign, in other words, can be accounted for and explained in terms other than itself, whereas a symbol speaks for itself. This has considerable implications for the way we use and handle sacramental symbols in the worshipping assembly. A symbol, because of its intrinsic multivalency, evades any attempt to decode or fix its meaning with any degree of propositional precision. The baptismal water, for instance, can trigger a range of associations, recalling biblical narratives like the creation myth of Genesis chapter 1, where formless water features as a symbol of fecundity; the flood narrative in Genesis chapter 7, where water is a symbol of dissolution and destruction; and stories like the Exodus through the Red Sea and the crossing of the river Jordan, where the waters mark a threshold which needs to be crossed in order to attain a fuller life and larger freedom. As well as evoking such a range of biblical meanings and motifs, the symbol of water also elicits and invites a range of emotional responses and stances: the feeling of fear unleashed by the dangers of water; the feeling of wonder elicited by the blood and water of a new birth; the feeling of

expectancy and anticipation at having crossed a perceived threshold into a new phase of life.

However, the potential of the sacramental symbol is not dissipated by the wide range of associations and responses that it can engender, but is focused in its power to create new possibilities for human existence and to depict deeper realities. In baptism, for example, the possibility of entering into the life of the divine Trinity and living within the community of faith is opened up for us; a possibility, furthermore, which is presented afresh each time Christians assemble to make and offer the eucharist. Now if sacramental symbols do indeed communicate and manifest such stupendous realities, then they cannot be meagre in themselves, or handled as if they were mere tokens. In our liturgical celebrations symbols should be ample, and expressively handled. So in the eucharist, the bread should be big enough to be broken, and then distributed in communion; in celebrations of baptism, the font should contain a sufficient volume of water in order that the infant may be dipped, or that water may be lavishly poured over the candidate; and in the anointing with holy oils, sufficient oil should be used, so that it is literally felt and its aroma smelt by the person being anointed. Sacramental symbols should show something of the prodigal generosity of divine grace, and those who preside at sacramental celebrations should appreciate that ample symbols require demonstrative symbolic actions and ritual gestures. Anointing needs to be a real pouring of oil and not a clinical dabbing; baptism a real drenching; and the fraction, the breaking of bread, a real and necessary practical preliminary to the distribution of the eucharistic gifts at communion. All these sacramental symbols should be handled in such a way that they have their full dramatic impact upon those who have gathered for the liturgical celebration, so that we may be more ready to change and be changed, as God transforms this world into his glorious kingdom.

Forms and prospects

Having examined the basic liturgical components of words, symbols and symbolic gestures, it would be appropriate to add at this juncture some reflections on possible forms and prospects. The comments I intend to make, however, should be read as a contribution to discussion, as the Church of England moves ever closer to another intensive phase of liturgical revision, rather than as definite proposals.

An area which requires some attention is the provision of alternative eucharistic prayers in the Communion service. The eucharistic prayer stands at the very heart of the Church's prayer, and constitutes the core of the whole eucharistic liturgy. It has been observed that the four eucharistic prayers in the Rite A Communion service of the ASB do not really provide the degree of variation which is found in the modern language rites of other

Provinces of the Anglican Communion. Indeed, the first three eucharistic prayers in Rite A of the ASB are similar in tone, structure and style, and share a common parentage, being modelled in varying degrees on the eucharistic prayer ascribed to Hippolytus, which is found in the third-century document called *The Apostolic Tradition*. This eucharistic prayer, generally taken to be the earliest fixed written eucharistic prayer, was seized upon by liturgical scholars in the 1960s and came to be regarded as the apogee of eucharistic praying. But scholarship in this field has moved on considerably. It is now generally appreciated that there was considerable regional variation in liturgical practice and patterns of prayer in the early Christian world. Furthermore, the very status of the so-called Hippolytan prayer (written, incidentally for the occasion of an ordination of a bishop, rather than the regular Sunday assembly) has been seriously questioned. The consensus now is that the prayer cannot be regarded as reflecting general practice in third-century Rome.

The fourth eucharistic prayer in Rite A is simply a recasting in contemporary language of material drawn from the *Book of Common Prayer* Communion service, and cannot therefore be regarded as a real alternative prayer. The alternatives, therefore, at least from a structural and stylistic point of view, turn out to be much of a muchness. An interesting contrast appears when they are compared to the eucharistic prayers (not authorised for use) in the Liturgical Commission's report *Patterns for Worship* (Church House Publishing 1989). Prayer C in that report is particularly interesting. It was largely inspired by an ancient East Syrian anaphora (eucharistic prayer) and is creatively written in a rich and suggestive vocabulary. Apart from the refreshing contrast in structure, the difference in vocabulary and tone between Prayer C and the three prayers of Rite A is quite revealing. But the point is probably best made anecdotally. A chaplain to the deaf has ventured the opinion that the main weakness of the eucharistic prayers in the ASB Rite A is their lack of pictorial language. Apart from the Hippolytan phrase, 'He opened wide his arms for us on the cross', the language is bald and abstractly conceptual. Needless to say, such abstract language is the most difficult to express in sign language.

The quality of our eucharistic prayers might well be enhanced if they were cast more deliberately in the form of narrative, rehearsing in 'story' form what God has done and continues to do and be for his people through Christ and in the Holy Spirit, rather than in the form of a series of credal sounding phrases. Historically the Western Church became accustomed to terse and economically expressed eucharistic prayers through the Latin Roman canon, although a varied repertoire of prayers survived in local rites such as the Mozarabic (Spanish) and Ambrosian (Milanese). By way of contrast, the eucharistic prayers of the Eastern Churches generally recapitulate in narrative form God's creative and redemptive work. The prayers are often prolix and weave together a number of biblical themes and figures. A contemporary attempt to construct such a prayer, covering the full sweep of what might be called 'salvation history', is to be found in Rite 2 of the American Episcopalian Church's *Book of Common Prayer* (1979). Prayer 'D' in this rite makes mention of how humanity, although created in the image of God, seeks to go its own way apart from God; rehearses how God entered into a covenant with his ancient people (a crucial reference point for the mention of the 'new covenant' in the Institution narrative), and how he recalled his people to the ways of justice and mercy through the prophets. This narrative reaches a crescendo in its Christological section, celebrating the incarnation and the earthly ministry of Jesus, his suffering, sending of the Spirit, death and vindication. The comprehensive recital of the creative and redemptive work of God expressed in this eucharistic prayer effectively locates the assembled worshippers within the context of God's saving purposes, and thus enables them to see themselves as standing in continuity with all God's people in every time and place.

The sweeping narrative in Prayer D of the ECUSA Prayer Book gives, as we have seen, adequate attention to the theme of God's work of creation. In the third eucharistic prayer of ASB Rite A, the theme of creation is condensed into a subordinate Christological clause: 'through whom you have created all things'. At a time when people are so conscious of ecological concerns, perhaps this theme requires a fuller treatment. After all, ample testimony is given to this theme in the earliest witnesses to the church's liturgical life and prayer. Justin Martyr, writing in AD150 to explain Christian practices in order to dispel gossip and misunderstanding, spoke of Christians 'offering prayers and hymns for our creation and all the means of well-being, for the variety of creatures and the changing of the seasons' (1 *Apology*, sec. 13), proof positive, if any was needed, that the Christian outlook is not to recoil from, but to embrace and affirm the natural conditions of human existence. Towards the end of the second century Irenaeus of Lyons, writing to counter the 'heretical' view which disdained the material world and over-spiritualised Christianity, spoke of the bread and wine brought for the eucharist as an offering of the first fruits of creation. In this way, he linked together elements of the natural world and products of human labour with the Christian sacrifice, and thereby implied that Christian redemption is the renewal and remaking of creation. For the place of this theme in the context of a eucharistic prayer, one might look to the eucharistic prayer in Book 8 of the fourth-century Syrian Church order, the *Apostolic Constitutions*, where there is a florid and almost rhapsodic account of the natural world and the varied plant and animal life it sustains. The Jerusalem Liturgy ascribed to St James, containing material which probably dates back to the fourth century, clearly views humanity as being a part of, rather than apart from, the natural world, in its assertion that creation voices its praise to God, as worshippers add their voice to that of the angels and archangels in the trisagion: 'Holy, Holy, Holy, Lord God Almighty, Heaven and earth are full of his glory.'

Driven by the weight of this tradition and by the concerns and preoccupations of our own times, we would do well to give much fuller expression to the theme of creation in our eucharistic praying, and the motif should certainly feature in the texts of those prayers which will be composed to replace or supplement the provision of the eucharistic prayers in the *Alternative Service Book (1980)*.

The kind of narrative eucharistic prayer which I have advocated in this section would undoubtedly produce a longer prayer than we are used to and could well exacerbate the problem, revealed by some recent research, that a number of people in our congregations switch off, or allow their attention to wander during that prayer, which ironically is the heart of the liturgy. One possible solution to the problem would be to maximise the responsorial character of the prayer with the insertion of general acclamations after each of its sections. Good examples of such eucharistic prayers can be seen in *Patterns for Worship*, but the difficulty with this arrangement is that it can interrupt the narrative flow and unity of the prayer. Perhaps the problem needs to be tackled in other ways, or seen as a challenge to liturgical catechesis, of how we help people to enter more deeply and understand what is said and done in the work of worship. The particular need is to convey to worshippers the fact that the eucharistic prayer is the prayer of the whole worshipping assembly, and impress upon those who preside at the eucharist that their voice, gestures and general attitude in the performance of that prayer should clearly signal that fact, and in no way suggest that it is the priest's 'magic bit'. Matters might also be improved if the eucharistic prayer was perceived by the worshippers as literally occupying the centre of the liturgy. To illustrate what I have in mind, I know of one church where worshippers sometimes feel that 'the ministry of the sacrament' is tacked on at the end of the service. Care should be taken to ensure that notices, the sermon and intercessions are not verbose to the point of unsettling the complementary balance of word and sacrament, and in any case the eucharistic prayer itself and the communion rite should never be hurried or rushed. Perhaps, too, consideration could be given to the question of streamlining the rite and possibly re-apportioning some of its material.

The whole eucharistic rite at a Sunday celebration could open with the greeting and move straight away into the Gloria in Excelsis, and then the collect for the day. The readings could follow according to the familiar pattern, and the sermon be followed by the intercessions, and (perhaps in Advent and Lent only?) prayers of penitence. The penitential rite could be so composed as to lead naturally into the peace, with the absolution, the declaration of forgiveness, structurally unfolding into the peace, as in the following example based on an alternative form from *A New Zealand Prayer Book* (1989):

> God forgives you and sets you free.
> Forgive others; forgive yourself,
> and approach your God in peace.

The greeting and exchange of the peace could follow at this point, and then the bread and wine could be brought to the altar from the body of the church. Ideally, the congregation should stand and be able to see the gifts being taken and presented at the altar, because they are *their* gifts. A hymn, if required, could be sung after the presentation of the gifts. The most radical suggestion in this proposed outline of the liturgy is the omission of the Creed, and this requires some explanation.

The Creed was a comparatively late addition to the Mass, with Pope Benedict VIII being persuaded to include it in the Roman Rite in 1014. It had admittedly been introduced into the Mass in Spain in the sixth century, but in that case it was inserted after the eucharistic prayer and before the communion rite where it was intended to function as a kind of test of orthodoxy, effectively erecting a fence between the people and the altar. But the Creed as an affirmation of faith would be an unnecessary duplication in a rite where a fuller, narrative form of eucharistic prayer was being used – a prayer, that is, which rehearsed the ways in which the triune God relates and redeems his creation, and thereby reveals the trinitarian shape of Christian believing. This faith could be actively affirmed by the congregation through encouraging the whole assembly to say or sing the doxology at the end of the prayer.

Daily prayer

Recent years have seen a renewed interest in daily prayer, not solely as a canonical duty imposed upon the clergy, but as a daily gathering of Christians, as envisaged by Thomas Cranmer and evidenced by his rubric that the curate should toll the church bell for morning and evening prayer, to offer a 'common prayer' of praise and petition. This revival of interest in corporate daily prayer has been stimulated partly by the appearance on the Anglican scene of two recent works: *Company of Voices* (1988) by the monastic liturgist George Guiver; and *Celebrating Common Prayer*, a version of the Franciscan daily office adapted for more widespread use.[6]

The eucharist is properly understood as the anamnesis, the 'making present' of God's saving presence and purposes, but it is not generally appreciated that daily prayer too has its anamnetic purpose. At evening prayer, with the lighting of the lamps (the Lucernarium), worshippers offer praise for the inextinguishable light and life of God in Christ and pray for protection for themselves and for all the vulnerable and needy, as they enter the darkness of the night. At morning prayer, after the dawn of a new day, worshippers offer praise to God for raising his Son, the Sun of Justice, and ask that the Holy Spirit may so guide them through the hours of the day that they may themselves manifest God's sovereign love and mercy. This basic scheme of daily prayer, morning and evening, is made explicit in the opening prayers provided for Morning and Evening Prayer in *Celebrating Common Prayer*, so that the paschal mystery of Christ's death and resurrection is celebrated and made present in the morning and evening of each day. The natural cycle of night and day, darkness and light, is an analogue of Christ's death and resurrection; as one ancient Christian writer, Clement of Rome, put it: 'Day and night show us the resurrection; night sets, day rises; day departs, night comes.' This anamnetic aspect of daily prayer has to be held together with the more popular theological view of daily prayer as the 'sanctification of time'.

With this revival of interest in a renewed practice of corporate daily prayer, perhaps we need to review the place and practice of the daily mass, the hallmark of most self-consciously Catholic parishes. The custom of Orthodox churches is to celebrate the Divine Liturgy on Sundays and feast days only, and although I do not intend to suggest that we simply adopt this pattern, their practice throws into sharp relief the question of whether the whole eucharistic rite needs to be celebrated on every ordinary, ferial weekday. Perhaps in churches which actively encourage a daily corporate celebration of morning and evening prayer, it might be more suitable on ordinary ferial days to use a shorter Order of Communion. This would be similar to the Mass of the Presanctified, which in the West is celebrated only on Good Friday, but in the East on every Wednesday and Friday in Lent. In this case, communion would be taken from the reserved Sacrament, and the Office would essentially be an office of preparation. Such a liturgical arrangement could cater for those who are daily communicants, and replace the daily mass shibboleth, which perhaps has sprung more from individual priestly piety than from the inherent character and purpose of the eucharist, or the needs of the local community.

The Effects of Worship

In his poem 'Little Gidding', T. S. Eliot tells us that when we enter sacred precincts our purpose should not be to instruct ourselves, or inform curiosity, but to pray where prayer is valid. The same point could equally be applied to worship, the Church's prayer. For worship, by definition, is directed towards God, and our primary purpose in worship is not to gain a greater understanding of Christian beliefs, or to generate a sense of bonhomie with fellow worshippers, but to acknowledge God's glory, literally, to feel the weight of his presence in the world and his influence in the making of human history. It is to give voice to the prayer of Christ (Hebrews 7:25), that the whole creation may be freed from the grip of destructive forces and its bondage to decay (Romans 8:22ff.). Yet despite this understanding that worship should be directed towards and centred upon God, some forms of worship, especially those which resulted from the Reformation, have deliberately been composed to inculcate particular preconceived attitudes and doctrinal stances. Thus the often quoted principle of *lex orandi, lex credendi* is inverted so that a particular view of Christian life and a particular doctrinal system comes to determine the shape and content of the Church's prayer. Allowing particular beliefs to determine the character and content of worship has the unfortunate consequence of suggesting that the primary purpose of worship is instruction.

What might fairly be described as the pedagogical view of worship was enshrined in the *Book of Common Prayer*. The original preface of the first English prayer books of Thomas Cranmer was taken up into the notes 'Concerning the Service of the Church', in the 1662 Prayer Book. In these notes it is expressly stated that the purpose of worship was that the clergy 'be stirred up to godliness themselves, and be more able to exhort others by wholesome doctrine, and to confute them that were adversaries to the truth', and that through their attendance at common prayer, the people themselves (by daily hearing of holy Scripture read in the Church) 'might continually profit more and more in the knowledge of God, and be the more inflamed with the love of his true Religion'. With such a strongly stated pedagogical purpose, and recalling the various prolix exhortations scattered through the Prayer Book, it is not surprising that a great deal of parochial worship in the Church of England has suffered by being over-didactic. Unfortunately, the more recent manifestations of didactic worship may well prove to be even more misguided, in so far as it may obscure the primary purpose of worship and obstruct the proper effect it should have upon its participants. For if, at least historically speaking, Anglican worship has been dogged by didacticism, the contemporary display of certain liturgical ministers, who seem to adopt the style of the TV chat show compere, reveals a form of didacticism which shades into a kind of religious entertainment. This all can trivialise too easily the serious 'play' of worship, the making present of heaven on earth. What is needed is neither triviality, nor on the other hand the suppression of our humanity, but that solemn informality which befits what might be called 'sacramental theatre'. We need to distinguish between dramatic worship and cheap theatricality. This is well illustrated by an experience at a wedding where the officiating minister, a well intentioned and good pastor, suffered from a virtual compulsion to comment on the set prayers and ritual actions. His declaration, 'Haven't they done well!' after the exchange of promises elicited embarrassed giggles from the congregation and effectively dispelled the sense of atmosphere and attention at that poignant moment in the marriage rite.

Real Presences

The significant effects of worship become apparent when we explore the notion of presence, and ask what it means to be present. At the immediate level, to cross the threshold into the church building and join with the assembled worshippers is to enter into the covenanted presence of God: 'Where two or three are gathered together in my name, I am there in your midst.' The depth and intensity of that presence is mediated and unfolded in the words, actions and symbols of the liturgy itself, which is at one and the same time both our action and the action of God. But unlike magic, which seeks to unleash and manipulate some kind of 'higher power', the power of God and the presence of the divine mystery can only touch and influence the worshipper in so far as he or she is present to that mystery. Being present, of course, involves more than simply being there, being physically present. Being present means being attentive, alert and open to the influence of God, and having the expectation that one will be changed by and through that encounter. This is precisely what is meant when people speak of the need for our 'faithful participation' in the church's worship. So, one could say that what is required from those who would worship is that they are fully present to the presence of the Other, the unfolding mystery of God. In purely human terms we know from experience what it means to meet and truly communicate with another human being, and how easily and all too frequently a meeting even with a friend or colleague is less than it could be. We might think of those occasions when we are led to say, 'We didn't connect'; those meetings when we might say of the other, 'He didn't really hear what I was saying'; or the scenario where another person is physically present, but 'not really with us'. Such frustrating and unsatisfactory encounters remind us that presence is more than proximity, and may sometimes require diligence and conscious effort. Being present with and for another is the bedrock of all real relationships with others and with God, for being present is not simply being there, being with another, but being *for* that person. As such it is the pre-condition of mutuality, of the reciprocal sharing of life and love.

What is required of the worshipper is an attentive, expectant presence before the Presence of the divine mystery, the mystery which unfolds before, within and between the worshippers, transforming them into the Body of Christ and suffusing each local body of worshippers with the life, light and energies of God. For it is the liturgical action which constitutes and makes the Church, and this is the primary and most significant effect of worship.

In one sense there is something monotonous about liturgical, fixed forms of worship, and the seemingly endless cycle of the liturgical year, year after year, but this feeling of sameness which worshippers might feel from time to time can serve a positive function. It can remind us that there is a limit to our powers of creative innovation, and perhaps more importantly, remind us that worship is not the projection of our religious 'feeling state', but something 'given', something repeatedly said and done which we ought to be open to, and need to respond to. Indeed, it could be argued, following the threads I have indicated above, that the very repetition of set forms of prayer and ritual enactments actually invites and draws the worshipper into the deep rhythm and grammar of the Church's prayer, which is the encounter with her Lord, and a communion with the ultimate mystery, the triune love of the Father, the Son and the Holy Spirit. Our faithful participation in the worship of the Church 'fashions and forms us' as Christians in and for the salvation of the world. In baptism, again to use a phrase of Casel, we are 'plunged into the paschal mystery of Christ', that we may live no longer for ourselves, but discover a new corporate identity and purpose as the people of God, empowered by the Spirit to declare in word and action God's coming Kingdom. Christians are pre-eminently sustained and constantly renewed in the living of the Christian life by their common offering of the eucharist and by receiving the gifts of communion; a fact which was perfectly caught by Thomas Cranmer in the beautifully crafted post-communion prayer in the English prayer books:

> Almighty and everliving God, we most heartily thank thee, for that thou dost vouchsafe to feed us, who have duly received these holy mysteries, with the spiritual food of the most precious Body and Blood of thy Son ... and dost assure us thereby of thy favour and goodness towards us; and that we are very members *incorporate* in the mystical body of thy Son.

The essential 'givenness' of the liturgy which I have alluded to here is probably most clearly seen and most keenly felt in the celebration of infant baptism. For with the baptism of infants, that is with those who are unable to talk their way into the church or a relationship with God, the rite publicly declares them to be children of God, and the worshipping community can only acknowledge God's initiative and work and welcome and receive the newly baptised as a 'gift'. (Incidentally, the exchange of the peace at a baptismal eucharist is an opportunity to sharpen awareness that within the eucharistic community we are each a 'gift' to each other.) But the 'givenness' of the liturgy is most supremely shown at that moment when the worshipper stands or kneels before the altar with open hands to receive the eucharistic gifts. In these gifts, these 'holy mysteries', the worshippers receive Christ's very being and life, so that in all the areas of their lives and in the many activities in which they are engaged they might be bearers of Christ, and thereby be bringers of hope and creators of conviviality.

Finally, the point of all that I have been attempting to say about the mystery of 'making present' was concisely and tellingly made by one who in his own life and ministry showed us that real liturgy is not the text on the liturgist's desk, but lived and prayed. In a now famous essay on the Parish Communion Michael Ramsey made this vital point: 'It is not a question of what we make of the eucharist, but of what it makes of us.'

Notes

[1] See *Model and Inspiration*, ed. M. Perham, (SPCK, 1993)

[2] R. Guardini, *The Spirit of the Liturgy* (Sheed and Ward, 1930), p. 84

[3] M. Douglas, *Natural Symbols* (Penguin, 1973)

[4] C. G. Jung, *Memories, Dreams, Reflections* (Fontana, 1967), p. 162

[5] A. Schmemann, *The Eucharist* (St. Vladimir Press, 1987), p. 38

[6] See also *Something Understood: A Companion to Celebrating Common Prayer*, eds. P. Roberts, D. Stancliffe, and K. Stevenson, and *Renewing Daily Prayer*, C. Cocksworth, and P. Roberts, Grove Worship Series, No. 123